ASFC LEARNING CENTRE

ESSENTIAL ART DECO

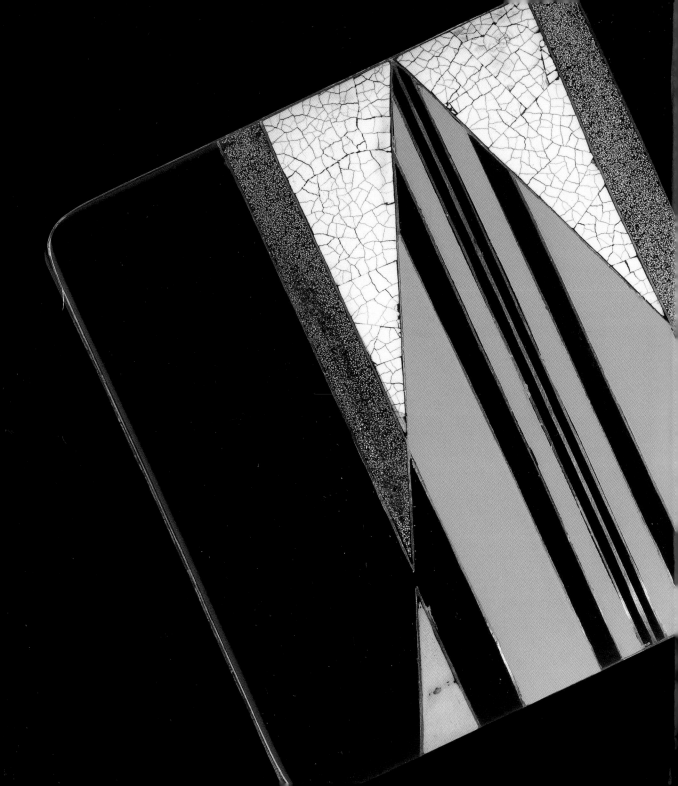

ESSENTIAL
ART DECO

GHISLAINE WOOD

V&A PUBLICATIONS

First published by V&A Publications, 2003
V&A Publications
160 Brompton Road
London SW3 1HW

Ghislaine Wood asserts her moral right to be
identified as the author of this book

Designed by Broadbase
V&A photography by Christine Smith, Mike Kitcatt
and Richard Davis of the V&A Photographic Studio

ISBN 1 85177 389 4

A catalogue record for this book is available from
the British Library

Front jacket illustration: Enoch Boulton, 'Jazz'
ginger jar. Earthenware painted in enamels and
gilt. Made by Wiltshaw & Robinson Ltd, Carlton
Works. British, 1928. V&A: Circ.526-1974.

Back jacket illustration: Jean Goulden, clock
(see plate 60).

Frontispiece: Gérard Sandoz, cigarette case.
Silver, enamel, lacquer and eggshell.
French, c.1929. V&A: Circ.329-1972.

Contents page: Donald Deskey, 'Lysistrata' screen.
Lacquer on wood and chrome. American, c.1930.
Xavier Roberts Collection.

Printed in Singapore

V&A Publications
160 Brompton Road
London SW3 1HW
www.vam.ac.uk

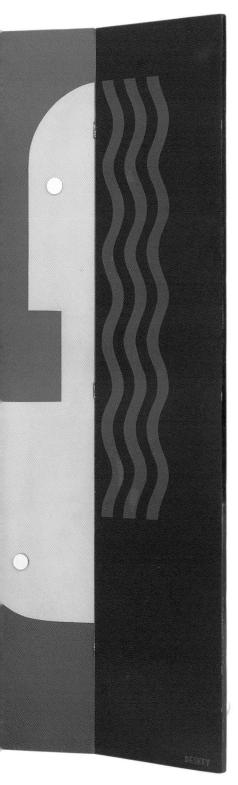

CONTENTS

INTRODUCTION

Art Deco is perhaps best understood as the style of an age of extremes. Spanning the boom of the roaring twenties and the bust of the Depression-ridden thirties, it came to represent many things for many people. It was the style of the flapper girl and the factories of Fordism, the luxury ocean liner and the skyscraper, the fantasy world of Hollywood and the real world of the Harlem Renaissance. It could be deeply nationalistic and yet it spread like wild fire all over the world, dominating the skylines of cities from New York to Shanghai and sheathing offices and factories from London to Rio. It presented a return to tradition and simultaneously celebrated the mechanized, modern world. It embraced handcraft production and the machine, exclusive works of high art and new products in affordable materials (plates 1 to 4). It affected all forms of design, from the fine and decorative arts to fashion, film, photography, transport and product design, and reached beyond these to encompass literature, music and dance (plate 6). It was modern and it was everywhere.

The style emerged in the years before 1914 in many of the cities that had embraced Art Nouveau and its development accelerated in the aftermath of the First World War. It drew life from many sources: the art of ancient civilizations and of the avant-garde, the exoticism of the Ballets Russes, the motifs of French tradition and the imagery of the machine age. By the early 1920s Art Deco had come to represent the fast and new, the exotic and the sensual. It was a style shaped, in Scott Fitzgerald's words, by 'all the nervous energy stored up and unexpended in the War'.[1] And although its

1 ABOVE
John Raedecker, 'Amsterdam', sculpture. Carved wood. Dutch, 1927–8. In the former Town Hall, now Amsterdam Grand Hotel.
Stedelijk Museum, Amsterdam.

2 ABOVE
André Groult, chiffonier. Mahogany, ivory
and sharkskin. French, 1925.

Musée des Arts Décoratifs, Paris.

creators tended to avoid social idealism, the style clearly reflected the tensions of wider cultural politics. For many European nations, the horrors of the First World War precipitated a profound re-evaluation of national traditions and characteristics. This 'return to order', as it was known in France, informed the search for a reassuring, accessible and above all national modern style in many countries.

Nowhere was this more clearly illustrated than in the displays at the Paris *Exposition Internationale des Arts Décoratifs et Industriels Modernes* of 1925. It was at this exhibition, visited by over 16 million people, that the Art Deco style burst on to the world stage. The rules demanded that only modern art and design was to be shown and as a result hundreds of Deco works from many nations were displayed. Although the French exhibits dominated, numerous countries participated, including Britain, Austria, Holland, Poland, Czechoslovakia, Italy, Sweden, Denmark and Russia. The multifaceted nature of Art Deco can be seen in the diversity of works exhibited. For example the Austrian pavilion was co-ordinated by Josef Hoffmann and displayed works from the crafts workshops of the *Wiener Werkstätte* that were highly decorative and heavily indebted to traditional forms (plate 5). The Dutch exhibits revealed a fascination with the exotic and particularly the crafts of the Dutch colony of Indonesia (plate 7), while the Polish pavilion employed forms and motifs derived from folk art (plate 8). For each of these countries the search for a national idiom was paramount, and the development of Art Deco went hand in hand with the exploration of native traditions. Although these works may seem wildly different to our eyes, to the contemporary

3 ABOVE
René Lalique, box and cover. Bakelite.
French, *c.*1935.
V&A: C.15-1981.

4 RIGHT
Tamara de Lempicka, *Girl in a Green Dress.*
Oil on panel. French, *c.*1927.
Musée National d'Art Moderne, Centre Georges Pompidou, Paris.

5 BELOW
Josef Hoffmann, bowl, gilded metal.
Austrian, *c*.1924.
V&A: M.41-1972.

6 RIGHT
Paul Colin, 'Josephine Baker'. Plate from
Paul Colin, *Le Tumulte Noir.* Paris, 1927.
NAL.

visitor they would all have appeared to be strikingly modern. As one critic observed, 'All the works of art collected here show a family of resemblance which can not fail to be noticed by even the least prepared [visitor].'[2]

Beyond the national pavilion displays, grand spectacle did much to promote the style. From Lalique's enormous glass fountains to the coloured illuminations of buildings and bridges by night, the exhibition provided spectacular visions of the city (plate 10). The manipulation of light for dramatic effect became an important feature of the Art Deco style after 1925. But it was perhaps the fusion of Art Deco with shopping that proved the greatest legacy of Paris 1925. Fabulous Art Deco window displays for boutiques and department stores encouraged visitors, and particularly women, to consume in the shopping capital of the world. For Fernand Léger, 'the street [had] become a permanent spectacle of ever-increasing intensity'[3] and the excitement of the street was simulated throughout the exhibition with avenues and bridges crammed with boutiques. At 1925, the educative missions of previous Worlds' Fairs was replaced with a new and thoroughly modern dream: redemption through consumption.

The Paris exhibition established Art Deco as the most fashionable of modern styles and influenced a generation of designers and consumers world-wide. The new age of communications helped to disseminate the style. As the rich travelled the world in luxury on Art Deco ocean liners such as the *Normandie*, film and magazines transmitted Art Deco to a global audience. In nearly every country Art Deco was adopted as a way of embracing the modern and escaping restricting values. From Japan to India, the style transformed both the urban environment and the palaces of the rich. Much of post-earthquake Tokyo was rebuilt in the style, while in India, the Maharajah of Jodhpur built Umaid Bhawan, one of the most fantastic Art Deco residences ever conceived, with its vast swimming pool, streamlined bathrooms and exotic hunting lodge (plate 9). Executed by native craftsmen to European designs, the palace fused Western and Indian decorative schemes and demonstrated one of the great strengths of Art Deco as it spread around the globe. Deco was a style that could be naturalized and adapted to incorporate native decorative forms and iconography and thereby ease the transition to the modern in many regions of the world.

As well as transforming the palaces of the rich, Art Deco became the style of the new pleasure palaces – hotels, cocktail bars, ocean liners and cinemas. In this world Art Deco came to represent a new set of aspirations and desires – youth, glamour, fantasy and fun. These themes were also promoted through that great conduit for Art Deco: Hollywood film.

Nowhere did the style have a greater impact than in America. The Deco skyscrapers of Manhattan quickly became icons of the new style, symbolic of the individualism and democracy of American capitalism. Hollywood films regularly seen by more than 80 million people a week in

7 BELOW
Jaap Gidding, wool carpet.
Dutch, 1920.
Rijksmuseum, Amsterdam.

8 RIGHT
Józef Czajkowski, interior of the Polish Pavilion at the Paris 1925 Exhibition. The Studio, 1925.
NAL.

9 ABOVE
Swimming pool, Umaid Bhawan, Jodhpur, India, 1929–44.

10 RIGHT
The Eiffel Tower, illuminated by Citroën during the Paris 1925 Exhibition. Colour-tinted photograph. French, 1925.

the mid-1930s transmitted American values and ideals and eventually American style, in the form of Streamlining, world-wide. America became the exemplar of a young nation striking out to become a world power, and in an age still governed by the old Empires of Europe it was to America that many countries looked for forms resonant of a modern and independent age. The skyscraper and Streamlining provided those forms, and from the soaring towers of Cape Town to the streamlined buildings of Napier in New Zealand it was American Deco that dominated the 1930s and represented the exuberant culmination of the style. As Scott Fitzgerald stated in *The Jazz Age:* 'We were the most powerful nation. Who could tell us any longer what was fashionable and what was fun?'4

The enormous success of Art Deco is, in part, due to the fact that it proved the most malleable of styles. Without a defining doctrine or manifesto, the style fragmented, like a Cubist painting, to envelop the modern world at its most dynamic points – ocean liners, skyscrapers, automobiles, jazz and Hollywood film. All elements of the style were bound together on a canvas of common themes – the decorative, the commercial, the fashionable, the individualistic and the symbolic.

The term Art Deco was not coined until the 1960s, and at the time the style was known by a variety of names, including Zig-zag modern, Jazz modern, or simply Moderne. It is a style that has been defined in myriad ways, but perhaps the one certainty is that Art Deco defies attempts, both then and now, to constrain it, to limit the dream of fantasy, glamour and escape.

VUE DE NUIT
LA TOUR EIFFEL

THE ICONOGRAPHY OF ART DECO

••

Eclecticism is one of the defining features of Art Deco. The style drew on many disparate sources, developing a distinct iconography that evolved from the use of traditional forms and motifs in the 1910s and 1920s through to Streamlining in the 1930s. The plurality of Art Deco has made it hard to pin down, but also accounts for its unique ability to appeal to an extremely broad and varied audience across the world and across the decades.

An Art Deco object, whether it be a skyscraper, a couture dress or a Bakelite radio, might rely on one or combine several sources to create a complex and modern symbolism. For example, Eileen Gray's elegant 'Pirogue' day bed (c.1919–20) demonstrates the subtle use of different sources to create a thoroughly modern work (plate 11). It is deeply eclectic in both its form and materials. Derived from the shape of a Polynesian or Micronesian dug-out canoe, its handcrafted form is exotic but simultaneously refers back to the tradition of historic day beds of the Empire, Restauration and Louis Philippe periods. The clean lines, simple form and lack of applied decoration, however, pull the work in another direction. They suggest the simplification of form and decoration

sought by Modernist designers. Finally, the sensual treatment of surface and use of lacquer, a technique derived from Asia, draw the work firmly back into the realm of the exotic. The 'Pirogue' day bed is a fascinating object, clearly decorative and typically Art Deco in its elision of several references – the exotic, the traditional and the modern.

To take another example, the Chrysler Building in New York (1927–30) has become one of the most enduring symbols of modernity of the twentieth century, and yet it too combines the exotic, the traditional and the modern (plate 12). Its glistening steel dome and pinnacle, with chevron windows, recall the form

11 LEFT
Eileen Gray, 'Pirogue' day bed. Lacquered wood with silver leaf. French, c.1919–20.
Gift of Sydney and Francis Lewis. Virginia Museum of Fine Arts, Richmond.

12 RIGHT
William Van Alen, Chrysler Building. New York, 1927–30.

of a stepped pyramid or ziggurat, an architectural idiom in part derived from ancient Meso-American and Egyptian structures. Below the pyramid, at the 59th floor, giant eagles jut out over Manhattan, guardians of capitalism and the traditional symbol of America. Below these, winged hub caps add to the mix of traditional and modern iconography; they signify the Chrysler Car Corporation and clearly identify the building as a monument to corporate America. The fantasy of the exterior is continued in the rich and exotic decoration of the interior. Pink and brown marble covers the walls of the lobby, while ornate lotus flowers bloom over the lift doors, creating the impression of a modern-day temple.

The influence of Modernist principles is clear in the tower. With its lack of surface decoration and rectilinear geometry, the soaring structure suggests rationalism and social order. Like the 'Pirogue' day bed, the Chrysler Building is a deeply eclectic work, whose forms and decoration convey certain messages.

To take one last example, streamlined objects often incorporate references to different sources but most commonly use form itself to convey symbolism. The Ronson cigarette lighter is a work redolent with messages aimed to attract the potential consumer (plate 13). Its machine-made form subtly mimics that of a ship, train or car, and to heighten this association the lighter is given decorative speed lines, or 'speed whiskers', around the body and base.

The design cleverly plays on the association with chic symbols of modernity. By concentrating on essential form and making the monumental miniature, the design brings something beyond the reach of the average consumer into the realm of the consumable. It is a domestic product that nevertheless carries with it all the glamour and appeal of an ocean liner. Its desirability also works on more than one level. The form of the lighter demands to be handled, its visual and physical appeal strengthened through the glamorous treatment of surface finish and use of modern materials such as plastic. Although a functional object, the Ronson lighter's appeal is deeply symbolic.

These works represent three distinct approaches to the Art Deco style and all rely on the use of decoration, symbolism, glamour and fantasy. They also reveal tensions at work within the style: tensions between the modern and traditional, the functional and the symbolic, the handcrafted and the machine-produced. Most Art Deco objects represent this complexity, but despite this, the style does have a clear and identifiable iconography of motifs and forms. It is a repertoire that continually developed throughout the period and across the globe, in response to varying cultural and economic pressures, and saw an overall shift from surface and applied ornament of the first phase of Deco to the advent of Streamlining, where form itself became decorative, in the early 1930s.

13 RIGHT
Cigarette lighter, chromium-plated steel and white plastic. Made by Art Metal Works, Inc. for Ronson, Newark. American, c.1925.
V&A: Circ. 266-1971.

TRADITIONAL MOTIFS

●●●●●●●●●●●●●●●●●●●●●●●●●●●●●●●●●●●●●

One of the most distinctive features of
Art Deco in the 1910s and 1920s
was the style's dependence upon a
traditional range of ornament and
motifs. As a generation of designers
rejected the intense sinuosity of Art
Nouveau, the search began for a
more lyrical and gentle imagery,
familiar and reassuring in an age
recovering from the damage of the
First World War and experiencing the
instability of the increasing tempo of
modern life. Many French designers
turned to the bourgeois styles of the
Empire, Restauration and Louis
Philippe, while in the Germanic
countries Biedermeier fulfilled the need
for a tradition free from the exclusivity
of the aristocratic Louis styles favoured
by the Art Nouveau designers.
As early as 1912 the French critic
Guillaume Apollinaire observed:

'This year there is not a trace of the so
called art nouveau style. On the other
hand, we are now witnessing the
beginnings of a struggle between two
opposing tendencies in decoration
which cannot fail to be interesting. This
is the struggle between the sumptuous
decoration that jewellers already excel
in, and the domestic decoration that,

14 OPPOSITE
Georges Lepape, plate from *Les
Choses de Paul Poiret*. French,
c.1911.

15 LEFT
Stéphany, for Jacques-Emile
Ruhlmann, wall covering of woven
silk and cotton. French, 1925.
Musée Historique des Tissus, Lyon.

16 BELOW
Süe et Mare, detail of a frieze
from *Interiors de Süe et Mare*.
French, *c*.1924.
NAL.

17 ABOVE
Robert Bonfils, binding for Henri de Régnier,
Les Rencontres de M. Bréot. Morocco with
morocco inlays and onlays, gilt and blind
tooling. French, 1919.
NAL.

18 LEFT
Van Cleef & Arpels, brooch with yellow
and white brilliant-cut and baguette
diamonds, rubies, emeralds and
sapphires set in platinum and gold.
French, c.1930.
V&A: M.142-1978.

19 RIGHT
Jacques-Emile Ruhlmann, dressing-
table. Oak with amaranth and
mahogany veneer. French, 1925.
V&A: W.14-1980.

20 BELOW
Paul Manship, *The Flight of Europa*. Bronze.
American, 1925.
Collection Lionel and Geraldine Sterling.

21 RIGHT
Carl Milles, *Dancing Maenad*. Bronze.
Swedish, 1912.
Carl Milles Museum, Stockholm.

returning to the tradition of the Louis-Philippe period (the last period to have produced a genuinely beautiful style of furniture), is directed only toward forging an original style for our time.'[5]

This new group of French designers, led by amongst others André Vera, André Mare, Louis Süe, André Groult, Paul Poiret and Jacques-Emile Ruhlmann, aimed to create a style that could stand alongside the great French styles of the past, to modernize tradition rather than abandon it. They particularly favoured architectural forms and motifs, often derived from the classical world, and also looked to motifs used in Western traditions. Urns or baskets of flowers, swags, garlands, fluted columns, pilasters, lyre forms and sculptural reliefs were commonly seen in all forms of decoration (plates 14 to 19).

Much of this imagery came with a long and varied history of treatment, and none more so than the female nude. The Art Deco nude was given a thoroughly modern treatment. Painters

such as Jean Dupas and Raphael Delorme elongated the female form to create highly stylized images reminiscent of Mannerist painting (plate 22). Sculptors also experimented with the classical nude, both as free-standing sculptures and as a motif in relief decoration. Alfred Janniot, Henri Bernard, Jaroslav Horejc, Carl Milles and Paul Manship elongated and distorted the female form and frequently explored classical subjects such as the Flight of Europa or Pallas Athena (plates 20, 21 and 23). It was not just in painting and sculpture that the classical figure made an appearance. In fact figuration was central to Art Deco practice, and myriad reclining nudes, dancing maenads or huntresses could be seen on everything from textile and poster designs, to moulded glass and ceramic vessels (plates 24 and 25).

22 LEFT
Jean Dupas, *Les Perruches*. Oil on canvas. French, 1925.
Xavier Roberts Collection.

23 RIGHT
Jaroslav Horejc, Pallas Athena. Painted, carved and gilt wood. Czech, 1920.
UPM – Museum of Decorative Arts, Prague.

24 LEFT
René Lalique, Bacchantes vase. Glass.
French, 1927.
V&A: Circ.379-1970.

25 RIGHT
Wilhelm Kåge, Argenta vase. Stoneware
inlaid with silver. Swedish, c.1930.
V&A: C.129-1984.

CUBIST ROSE

26 LEFT
Detail from Paul Follot, dressing-table.
Carved gilt and lacquered wood.
French, 1919–20.

Musée d'Art Moderne de la Ville de Paris.

27 RIGHT
Mannequin (probably Siégel) wearing a
cloche hat by Kilpin Ltd. Pink straw with
appliqué trim. French and British, 1925.

V&A: T.442-1977; T.3-2002.

STYLIZED NATURE

To the imagery derived from the classical world and the high styles of European tradition were added new motifs in the 1920s. Nature, the prime subject of Art Nouveau, continued to provide inspiration and a rich source of forms for the Deco designers, but its treatment clearly shows the paradigmatic shift between the two styles.

The Art Nouveau designers embraced nature as a progressive model for the development of a new style; its vital energy and constant evolution was to be emulated. Yet the combination of the mystical importance of nature and its Darwinian drive, central to the evolution of Art Nouveau, was lost on the Art Deco generation. For them nature was to be flattened and mechanized and made appropriate for the modern machine world. In Art Nouveau the asymmetry of nature was celebrated, whereas in Art Deco conventionality and symmetry were imposed. Although it could be argued that the move towards a simplification of natural motifs was driven by the need to create decorative forms achievable in machine production, the shift from the organic and metaphoric in Art

Nouveau to the stylized and formalized in Art Deco represents a move towards conservatism.

Perhaps the best example of the way Art Deco controlled and modified nature is seen in the treatment of the Cubist rose. Although often used in handcrafted objects, the Cubist rose suggested machine production, with its angular forms and machined aesthetic. It appeared on everything from furniture and architecture to jewellery and fashion and became one of the most identifiable motifs of the new style (plate 27). Alongside the Cubist rose, floral imagery became extremely popular. Simplified and stylized flower and foliage patterns, often incorporating birds and animals, were extensively used in all forms of design but were particularly prevalent in textile design. They were most often executed in the bright, bold colours that are so typical of the early phase of Art Deco. A number of English textile manufacturers produced floral prints, including the companies of Grafton and Foxton (plate 28). These companies employed young designers such as Minnie McLeish to modernize

FLOWERS

28 OPPOSITE
Minnie McLeish, furnishing fabric. Roller-printed cotton. Made by William Foxton Ltd.
British, 1925.
V&A: Circ.628-1956.

29 LEFT
Henri Rapin and Anne-Marie Fontaine, vase and cover. Porcelain painted in enamels.
Made by the Manufacture de Sèvres.
French, c.1925–33.
V&A: C.116-1992.

30 ABOVE
Raoul Dufy, furnishing fabric in printed linen.
Made by Bianchini-Férier. French, 1920.
V&A: Misc.2:29-1934.

their output. Some of the strongest Deco textile designs were produced by the French company of Bianchini-Férier, who commissioned the Fauvist painter Raoul Dufy to design a series of modern patterns. Many of Dufy's designs employed lush floral and animal motifs in strong colours (plate 30). Another motif drawn from nature and frequently used in the 1920s was the leaping deer or antelope which in profile presented a strong outline that could be easily adapted for machine production. Motifs such as the leaping deer, in fact an ancient form in both Europe and Asia, were again given a highly stylized treatment to clearly signify them as modern symbols (plates 31 and 32). The Japanese lacquer artist Ban'ura Shōgo encapsulated the energy of the modern world with his dynamic partition screen, where the leaping deer merges with the flux of its surroundings. The most distinctive new motifs drawn from nature to be added to the repertoire in the 1920s were the

LEAPING DEER

31 LEFT
Marcel Goupy, vase. Blown glass with opaque and translucent enamels and gilding. Made by Maison Rouard. French, c.1925.
V&A: C.258-1987.

32 RIGHT
Ban'ura Shōgo, partition screen. Lacquer on wood. Japanese, 1930.
Private Collection.

FOUNTAIN, SUNBURST AND LIGHTNING BOLT

33 ABOVE
Walter Gilbert, frieze panel. Cast and painted aluminium. Made by the Bromsgrove Guild for Derry and Toms Building, London. British, 1933.
V&A: M.262-1984.

34 RIGHT
Clarice Cliff, 'Sunray' vase. Earthenware, painted in enamels. Made by Arthur J. Wilkinson, Ltd. British, c.1929–30.
V&A: C.74-1976.

frozen fountain, the sunburst and the lightning bolt. Again, these were motifs resonant of the dynamism of the modern world but made acceptable and reassuring through stylization and symmetry (plates 33 to 35).

In many countries, forms and motifs drawn from nature could easily be adapted and naturalized to serve distinctly national or regional needs. Native flora and fauna replaced classical ornamentation in countries keen to assert their cultural independence. For example, motifs such as the moose and beaver in Canada, or the goanna and duck-billed platypus in Australia, fed the search for a national iconography, their appeal heightened by the lack of stylistic convention associated with their treatment (plate 36).

35 BELOW
Tea service. Earthenware, painted in
enamels. Made by Gray's Pottery & Co Ltd.
British, c.1935.
V&A: C.295-1976.

36 RIGHT
A platypus on a stained-glass window of
the National Film and Sound Archive in
Canberra. Australian, 1930.

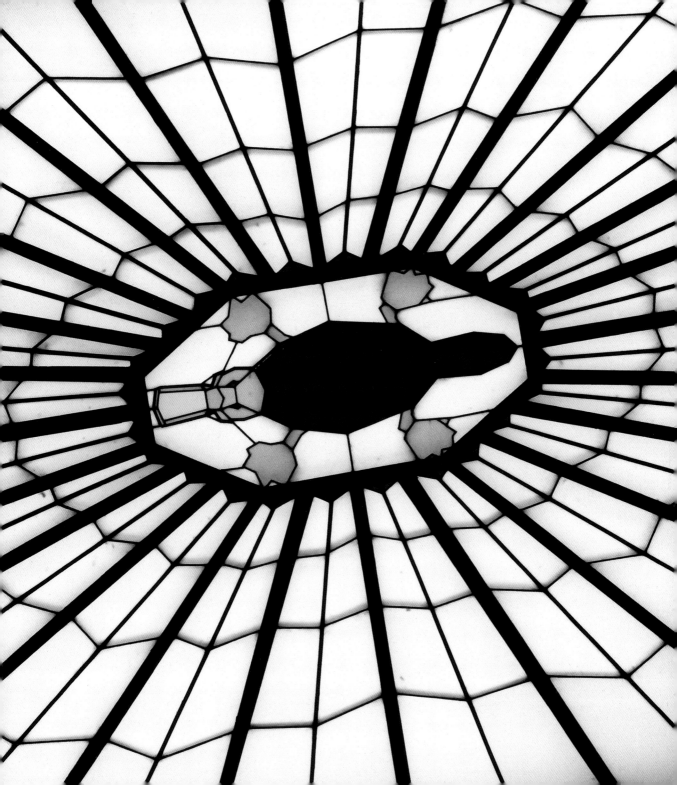

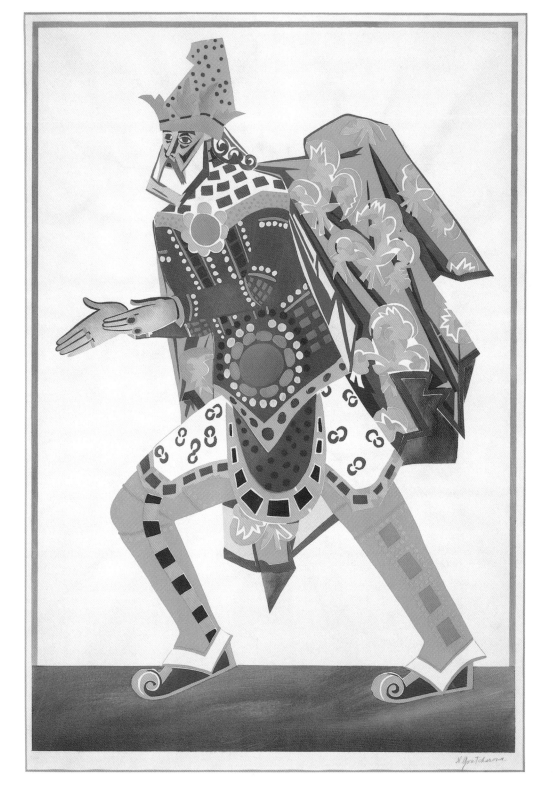

THE EXOTIC

••

Art Deco designers drew from many sources, but none gave the style its distinct flavour more than the exotic. Exotic imagery and motifs were plundered from many cultures. The arts of Africa and the Far East proved a rich source of forms and materials, while recent archaeological discoveries fuelled a romantic fascination with the ancient cultures of Egypt, Mesopotamia and Meso-America. The Ballets Russes synthesized many of these sources and represented them in a vital and modern experience, intensifying their power through the fusion of dance, music, colour and drama. The exotic provided a well-spring of forms and motifs for the renewal of style. In the words of a contemporary critic, describing the influence of African art, it was 'not a question of competing with the models of classical antiquity, but of renewing subjects and forms'.[6] Renewal became a distinguishing characteristic of Art Deco.

BALLETS RUSSES

37 LEFT
Natalia Goncharova, costume design for a magus in *Liturgie,* Ballets Russes. Stencil print on paper. Russian, 1915.
V&A: E.1112-1926.

EGYPT

38 BELOW
Bookbinding for Anatole France, *Balthasar,* Paris, 1926. Dark red calf with inlay of calf and niger of various colours; gilt and blind tooling. French, 1926.
NAL.

39 LEFT
Cartier, Egyptian temple gate clock. Gold,
silver gilt, mother-of-pearl, coral, enamel,
lapis lazuli, cornelian and emeralds.
French, 1927.
Cartier Collection, Geneva.

40 RIGHT
Sequin jacket with Egyptian motifs.
Hand-beaded lurex.
Probably French, c.1922–9.
V&A: T.91-1999.

The archaeological discovery that gripped the public imagination most profoundly was that of the tomb of the boy Pharaoh, Tutankhamun. In November 1922, Howard Carter uncovered an undisturbed tomb in the Valley of Kings near Luxor. It was to prove one of the most important discoveries in archaeological history. The riches extracted over the following months far outstripped both the public's and the archaeologist's expectations. Funerary goods included spectacular jewellery, chariots, furniture, alabaster vessels and the fantastic gold mask and mummy cases. The objects sparked enormous popular interest in all things Egyptian. It was, however, not so much the specific forms of the Tutankhamun pieces that were incorporated into Art Deco design, but rather generic Egyptian imagery such as lotus flowers and buds, scarabs and hieroglyphics. The pylon and the pyramid were particularly popular motifs and appeared in many forms of decorative arts, from bookbindings to jewellery. Indeed in some quarters, such as fashion design, the influence was quite tangential. The 'Mummy Wrap', a form of fashionable dress all the rage in the 1920s, evoked the layered bindings of the ancient mummies.

41 BELOW
George Cole, Carlton cinema, Essex Road, London, 1930.

42 ABOVE
Claudette Colbert in *Cleopatra*, directed
by Cecil B. De Mille, 1934.

The influence of the ancient cultures of Meso-America was also extremely significant, if not as obvious as that of Egypt. While Egyptian symbols and motifs were applied wholesale in Art Deco, the art of the Maya and Aztecs was adapted to create new architectural and decorative forms. The art of the ancient native peoples of Central and South America also provided a very particular source for the modern inhabitants of North America in the 1920s and 1930s. It represented an indigenous art free from traditional Western styles. For a country aiming to create a modern national identity, distinct from European culture, the architecture of Meso-America provided a bold and unadulterated source. The most significant impact of these cultures was on the architecture of North America. Stepping and set-backs, in part derived from ancient ziggurats, became common features

MESO-AMERICA

43 LEFT
Henri Sauvage, design for 'Métropolis',
pyramidal building in rue de Passy, Paris.
Gouache and gold ink on paper.
Fonds Documentaire IFA, Paris.

44 ABOVE
Lydia Bush-Brown Head, 'Temple of the
Mayan Indians'. Silk. American, 1926.
Gift of Mrs Francis Head. Cooper-Hewitt, National Design
Museum, Smithsonian Institution.

45 RIGHT
El Castillo, Chichen Itza, Yucatan,
Mexico, c.AD 800.

of the great skyscrapers of New York and other American cities.

The American textile designer Lydia Bush-Brown Head interestingly depicted both the Manhattan skyline and Mayan temples in her experimental exotic batik wall hangings. It is no accident that she chose these subject matters, as both were seen as fresh new symbols. Her Mayan temple hanging, executed in vibrant colours, included a highly exotic animal that was frequently depicted in Art Deco – the panther. Associated with the jungle, the panther, or jaguar, was a sacred animal to ancient Central and South American cultures but was transformed in Art Deco into the most exotic and elegant of modern beasts (plates 46 and 47).

The East, the exotic realm that traditionally fed Western fantasies, underwent some revision in the Art Deco period. The Islamic world, enormously influential in Art Nouveau, exerted less sway on the Deco designers. Although the Western fascination with the odalisques continued, the forms and motifs of Islamic design – the arabesque and the ogee – were not commonly used in Art Deco; nor were the sinuous floral patterns of Islamic textile and carpet design.

Japan, however, continued to exert a tremendous influence. In the late nineteenth century, as Japanese objects began to appear in the West, artists quickly absorbed the attributes of Japanese art. Decorative stylization, the use of bold, flat colour, strong outline and asymmetric composition were all present in Art Nouveau and were also used in Art Deco. But although Deco designers continued to borrow motifs – for example, Edgar Brandt's 'Les Cigognes d'Alsace' is derived from a traditional Japanese crane design – interest in the materials and techniques of Asia began to supersede style (plates 48 and 49). The increasing fascination with sensuality, luxury and rich surface finish led to a craze for lacquer. A traditional Asian technique, it became one of the most favoured of modern materials. Jean Dunand and Eileen Gray, two of the most celebrated Deco lacquer designers, learnt the technique from the Japanese master Sugawara Seizō, who had settled in Paris after the *Exposition Universelle* of 1900. The versatility of lacquer meant that it could be applied to wood, metal, leather and textiles and used for a variety of different objects, but it was perhaps used to greatest effect in the stunning furniture and screens created by both European designers and Japanese masters of the medium (plates 32 and 51).

In popular culture it was China that began to hold sway over the public appetite for fantasy and romance.

THE EAST

48 LEFT
Edgar Brandt, 'Les Cigognes d'Alsace' panel from a lift cage, Selfridges, London. Lacquer on metal on wood.
V&A: Circ. 719-1971.

49 RIGHT
Gift cover or 'fukusa'. Satin silk with silk embroidery. Japanese, nineteenth century.
V&A: T.20-1923.

Films such as *The Mask of Fu Manchu*
and Frank Capra's *The Bitter Tea of
General Yen* depicted the Chinese as
dangerous and inscrutable, but this
danger was fused with an attraction
for mysterious and forbidden pleasures.
In *The Bitter Tea of General Yen*, a
film banned in Britain for its depiction
of a cross-racial love affair, Barbara
Stanwyck rejected convention by
falling in love with the extremely
attractive but brutal Chinese war lord.
Adding to such romantic visions,
Chinese motifs and forms frequently
appeared in the fashions of the day.
Cartier produced a range of vanity
cases that employed Chinese motifs,
and even used materials associated
with the East such as lapis, onyx,
jade and coral. And the French
couturier Paquin created a spectacular
diamanté-covered flapper dress for the
Paris exhibition of 1925, decorated
with a central panel of blue silk
depicting dragons with sparkling eyes
and embroidered with pearls (plate 50).

50 RIGHT
Jeanne Paquin, 'Chimère' evening gown in
beaded silk. French, 1925.
V&A: T.50-1948.

51 ABOVE
Jacques-Emile Ruhlmann, Jean Dunand and
Jean Lambert-Rucki, detail of Donkey and
Hedgehog cabinet. Black lacquer with
incised silver decoration. French, 1925.
De Lorenzo, New York.

Africa was one of the richest sources of exotic imagery in Art Deco. The Deco designers took bold abstract and geometric patterns and the subdued black and brown colour range typical of Central African art. Derived from the patterns seen on African textiles, shields and sculptures, zig zags, hatch marks, circles and triangles became part of the repertoire of Art Deco motifs and were applied to everything from textiles and wallpapers to vases and jewellery (plate 54). Many Art Deco designers developed an iconography that used the African figure as a motif often set in lush jungle, while others began to explore the African sculptural tradition of masks. In France, Jean Lambert-Rucki and Pierre Legrain produced many African-inspired sculptures and pieces of furniture, while the Black American artist Sargent Johnson saw in African art the source of a racially conscious, modern decorative style (plates 53 and 55).

AFRICA

52 LEFT
Sigmund Pollitzer, panel in sand-blasted glass. Made by Pilkington Ltd. British, 1933–8.
V&A: C.230-1991.

53 RIGHT
Jean Dunand and Jean Lambert-Rucki, wooden chair. French, 1924.
Private Collection, Paris.

54 LEFT
René Buthaud, stoneware vase.
French, *c.*1920.
V&A: C.292-1987.

55 RIGHT
Sargent Johnson, mask. Copper with
ceramic inlay. American, *c.*1934.
Collection John P. Axelrod, Boston, MA.

GEOMETRY AND ABSTRACTION

••

Alongside traditional and exotic forms and motifs, designers also looked to the art of the avant-garde as a source of inspiration. Developments in the fine arts, from French Cubism and Orphism to German Expressionism, Italian Futurism and Russian Constructivism, provided designers with a fundamentally new and thoroughly modern pictorial language whose forms were derived from the imagery of the mechanized world (plate 56). For an artist such as Leger, the 'excitement and exaltation depended upon [a] peculiarly intense emotional reaction to mechanism, an emotion expressed . . . through his specific sense of geometric form'.[7] The movement towards geometry and abstraction that avant-garde art presented was quickly assimilated into the Deco style. For contemporary artists and designers alike, geometry represented a distillation of the modern world. Through the use of pure forms such as the circle, the square or the line, or through fragmenting form and plane, the dynamism of the modern world could be made into pattern.

56 RIGHT
**Fernand Léger, *Les Disques dans la Ville.*
Oil on canvas. French, 1920.**
Musée National d'Art Moderne, Centre Georges
Pompidou, Paris.

57 ABOVE
Sonia Delaunay, fashion drawing of
three women in hats and jackets.
Gouache on paper. French, c.1925.
V&A: E. 7-1980.

58 RIGHT
Ashtray in Bakelite, made by Roanoid
Ltd. British, c.1935.
V&A: C.54-1984.

59 OPPOSITE
Fortunato Depero, detail of tray
advertising Campari. Inlaid and
stained woods. Italian, 1927.
Private Collection, Trento.

Many avant-garde artists applied their ideas to design. Sonia Delaunay experimented with the juxtaposition of bright blocks of colour and geometric form in her fashion and textile designs, stating: 'There was no gap between my painting and my decorative work and...the minor art had never been an artistic frustration but a free expansion, a conquest of new space. It was an application of the same research'[8] (plate 57). The Italian Fortunato Depero applied the ideas of Futurism to advertising to promote products such as Campari (plate 59). However, little distinction was made between different avant-garde groups. All was seen as Cubism, which became a by-word for modern style and was applied almost randomly by contemporary critics to anything which appeared even vaguely modern.

The imagery of the avant-garde was used in a wide range of goods, from the most expensive jewellery and silverwork to cheap plastic objects such as boxes and ashtrays (plates 58, 60 and 61). Graphics and textile designs absorbed the new pictorial language most easily, and artists such

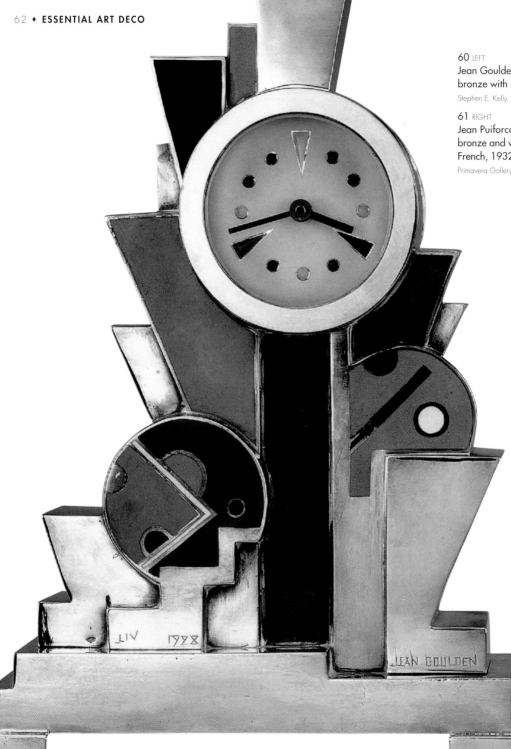

as Edward McKnight Kauffer did much to popularize this imagery in the commercial world of poster and book jacket design. However the lessons learnt from avant-garde art did not stop at the decorative arts and graphics; they also profoundly influenced architecture, interior design and photography (plates 67 to 69). The increasing emphasis on abstraction led to a paired down, spare approach to architecture and interiors that looked to line and surface rather than applied decoration for effect. This restraint, combined with the use of materials such as aluminium, chrome and glass and the increasingly sophisticated sculptural manipulation of light, led to some of the most glamorous and progressive interiors of the period.

62 LEFT
Pierre Chareau, textile in block-printed linen.
V&A: Misc.2:34-1934.

63 BELOW
Frank Lloyd Wright, dinner set in
porcelain, designed c.1922, made by
Noritake-Heinz & Co.
V&A: C.223-1984.

64 RIGHT
Edward McKnight Kauffer, wool
carpet. American, 1925.
V&A: T.440-1971.

65 RIGHT
Donald Deskey, screen. Wood, canvas,
paint and metal fittings. American, c.1930.
Collection John P. Axelrod, Boston, MA.

66 BELOW
Paul T. Frankl (born in Austria), hand mirror,
brush and comb set. Celluloid and mirrored
glass. American, 1930.
Collection John P. Axelrod, Boston, MA.

67 ABOVE
František Drtikol, *Composition* 1925.
Bromoil print, Czech, 1925.
UPM – Museum of Decorative Arts, Prague.

68 LEFT
Paul Nash, Tilly Losch bathroom.
British, 1932.
NAL.

69 ABOVE
Oliver Bernard, Foyer of the Strand Palace
Hotel, London 1930–31.

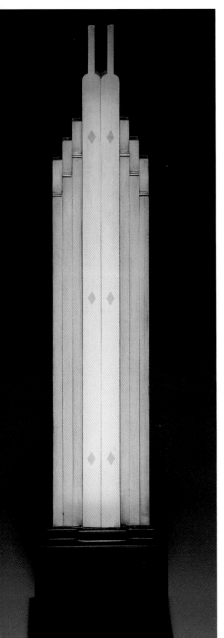

70 LEFT
John Storrs, *Forms in Space, Number 1.*
Stainless steel and copper. American,
c.1924.
M. Francis Lathrop Fund, 1967. The Metropolitan
Museum of Art, New York.

71 RIGHT
Joseph Stella, *Old Brooklyn Bridge.* Oil
on canvas. American, c.1941.
Gift of Susan Morse Hilles in memory of Paul Hellmuth.
Courtesy Museum of Fine Arts, Boston.

THE CITY AND
THE MACHINE
●●●

From the real skyscrapers of New York
to the fantasy skylines of the German
Expressionist film *Metropolis* (1926),
the city became one of the most
resonant symbols of modernity.
Innumerable films of the 1920s and
1930s used the city to denote a
modern world with new values and
lifestyles. Artists explored the
infrastructure of the city, its transport
systems, roads and bridges, to
symbolize an increasingly mechanized
and frenetic environment, while the
skyscraper became the most evocative
icon of the modern age. Art Deco
designers plundered this imagery in
search of a meaningful modern
iconography.

In many ways it was through the
eyes of outsiders that America began
to appreciate the awesome spectacle
of its skyscraper metropolis. The
German film director Fritz Lang
recounted his first impression of New
York by night:

'The view of New York…is a beacon
of beauty strong enough to be the
centrepiece of a film…there are
flashes of red and blue and gleaming
white, screaming green, streets full of
moving, turning, spiralling lights, and

high above the cars and elevated trains, skyscrapers appear in blue and gold, white and purple, and still higher above there are advertisements surpassing the stars with their light.'⁹

Whether for the émigré arriving in a new country and seeing the Manhattan skyline for the first time, or for the visitor such as Lang, New York presented an irresistible force and a symbol of progress and modernity. For one émigré, the Austrian designer Paul Frankl, 'the skyscraper was a more vital contribution to the field of modern art than all the things done in Europe put together'¹⁰. And Frankl was the first to use the skyscraper as a symbol of national identity and provide resonant modern American imagery in his range of 'Skyscraper' furniture (plate 72). Many American designers followed, exploring the city to create an original iconography. In Ruth

72 LEFT
Paul T. Frankl, desk and bookshelf. Walnut, paint and brass handles. American, c.1928.
Collection John P. Axelrod, Boston, MA.

73 RIGHT
Ruth Reeves, 'Manhattan' furnishing fabric. Block-printed cotton. American, 1930.
V&A: T.57-1932.

THE ROYAL MAIL LINE
TO
NEW YORK
MAKE YOUR NEXT CROSSING BY
"THE COMFORT ROUTE"
THE ROYAL MAIL STEAM PACKET CO
ATLANTIC HOUSE. MOORGATE. E.C.2

74 ABOVE
Horace Taylor, *The Royal Mail Line to New York*. Poster, colour lithograph. British, 1920–25.
V&A: E.516-1925.

Reeves' 'Manhattan' textile, the symbols of a modern world – the towers, the ships, the planes and bridges – collide in a Cubist collage that telescopes time and space (plate 73). The Gorham Manufacturing Company's silver 'Cubic' coffee service (1927), designed by another émigré, the Dane Erik Magnussen, indelibly fused the imagery of the city, the machine and the forms of Cubism (plate 75). One of the great works of American Art Deco, it became known as 'The Lights and Shadows of Manhattan'. It is a work that decoratively expresses the spirit of the machine age.

75 LEFT
Erik Magnussen, 'Cubic' coffee service
or 'The Lights and Shadows of Manhattan'.
Silver, silver gilt and oxidized silver.
Made by Gorham Manufacturing Co.
American, 1927.

Museum of Art, Rhode Island School of Design.
Gift of Textron Inc.

76 BELOW
Rene Paul Chambellan, entrance gates to
the executive suite of the Chanin building,
New York. Wrought iron and bronze.
American, 1928.

Gift of Mr Marcy Chanin. Cooper-Hewitt, National Design
Museum, Smithsonian Institution.

STREAMLINING

••••••••••••••••••••••••••••••••••••••

The 1930s witnessed the emergence of a new approach to design which, although not invented in America, took root and quickly became identified as a wholly American phenomenon. Streamlining transformed the look of everything, from factories and cinemas to transport, product, film and fashion design.

Responding to the demands of manufacturers – hit hard by the Depression – for a style that could be adapted to the production of cheap new products, a group of American designers developed an innovative approach to the process of design known as 'Styling'. Designers such as Norman Bel Geddes, Walter Dorwin Teague, Paul Frankl and Raymond Loewy began to encase products in contoured shells, the forms of which were derived from transport machines such as ocean liners, zeppelins, planes, trains and cars. The tubular, concave, convex, contoured and teardrop forms of Streamlining could be created using machine mass-production processes such as

77 RIGHT
Gordon Miller Buehrig, Auburn 851
'Boattail' speedster. American, 1935.
National Motor Museum, Beaulieu.

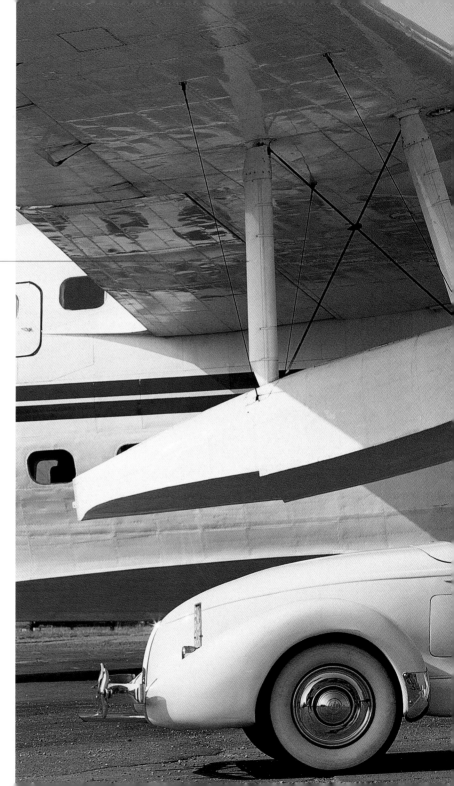

moulding, casting or dye stamping, and could be adapted for use in new materials such as plastics and aluminium. The visual appeal of Streamlining was heightened by the sensual treatment of surface finish and the embellishing of objects with 'speed whiskers', decorative lines that followed the contours of the work to suggest movement and speed.

Streamlining can be seen as yet another strategy to renew decoration. Rather than absorb new motifs or adapt the pictorial languages of the avant-garde, Streamlining turned to the very form of objects. Through the use of forms that metaphorically represented speed, progress and technology, Streamline design created works that were thoroughly modern and highly desirable. It lent glamour to the most mundane of domestic products and played upon consumers' desire for modern goods that represented the height of fashionable taste. Importantly, Streamlining also represented a modern American

78 LEFT
Raymond Loewy, prototype pencil sharpener. American, 1933.

79 RIGHT
Walter von Nessen, 'Coronet' coffee urn. Chrome-plated metal, plastic, glass. Made by Chase Brass & Copper Co. American, c.1930.
Collection John P. Axelrod, Boston, MA.

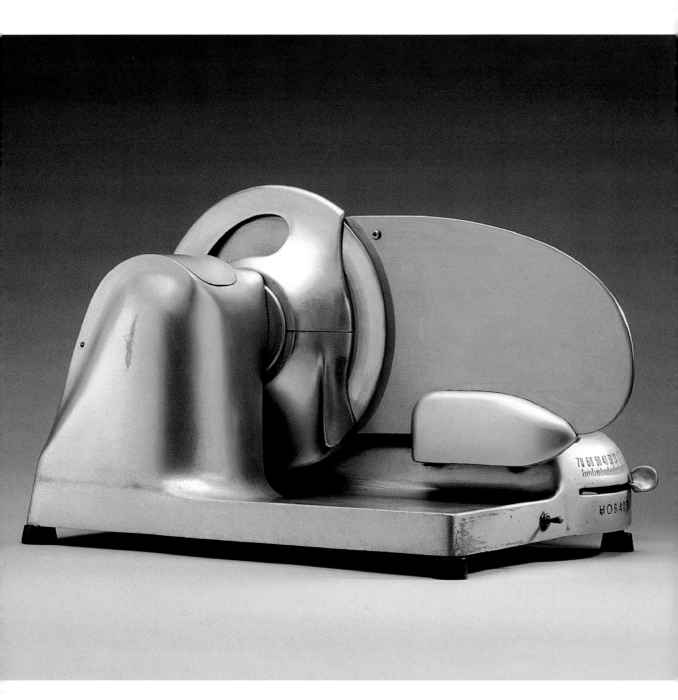

80 LEFT
Egmont Arens and Theodore C.
Brookhart, 'Streamliner' meat slicer.
Aluminium, steel and rubber. Made by
Hobart Manufacturing Company.
American, designed 1940,
manufactured 1944.

Gift of John C. Waddell, 2000. The Metropolitan
Museum of Art, New York.

81 RIGHT
Peter Müller-Munk, 'Normandie' water
pitcher in chrome-plated brass.
American, 1935.

Anonymous Gift, 1989. The Metropolitan Museum
of Art, New York.

idiom. A mark of its enormous success, Streamlining evolved from the particular circumstances of the Depression to become a style that by the late 1930s represented the vibrancy and mass appeal of American culture world-wide. Promoted through such agencies as Hollywood film, the effects of Streamlining were far-reaching, even altering the human form. In 1934, *Vogue* magazine reported that a fashionable woman's 'profile will have the windswept fleet lines of a speed boat or aeroplane'[11] (plate 85).

Streamlining marks the last phase of development of Art Deco. Its forms were deeply symbolic and highly decorative and aimed to stimulate consumption rather than facilitate function. As such, it is part of the rich story of Art Deco – the twentieth century's other modernism.

82 LEFT
Ocean Drive, South Beach, Miami.

83 ABOVE
Fada 'Bullet' streamliner radio, model 115.
American, 1940.
V&A: W.26-1992.

84 LEFT
John Vassos, portable phonograph, model
RCA Victor Special. Aluminium, chrome-
plated steel, plastic and velvet. American,
c.1937.
V&A: W.1-1997.

85 RIGHT
Charles James, evening gown in black satin.
British, 1936–37.
V&A: T.290-1978.

CONCLUSION

••

The rampant consumerism and individualism represented by the New York World's Fair of 1939 marked the culmination of Art Deco. Its streamlined and geometric buildings glorified capitalism and celebrated the American dream in the face of totalitarianism and war in Europe.

The post-war world was very different. It was a world of austerity, rationalism and powerful functionalist dogmas. Principal among these was the idea that ornament was unnecessary, or in the words of Modernist critic Herbert Read, 'should be treated as suspect'. In the reconstruction of the infrastructure of society – the housing estates, hospitals and schools – Utopian agendas were to rule and the flamboyance and 'sham splendour' of Art Deco fell deeply out of favour. Indeed, it was seen as no more than an aberration by the high Modernist critics, who excised it from the history of twentieth-century art and design.

However, Art Deco is still very much with us today. The 1960s saw a revival of interest which quickened in pace in the 1980s as a new generation of designers and architects explored Deco's decorative forms and motifs. For the last twenty years designers have continually returned to Art Deco as a source of inspiration.

A multifaceted style, Art Deco reflects the plurality of the modern world. But more than this, Art Deco responds to the human need for pleasure and escape. Ironically, by celebrating the ephemeral, Art Deco succeeded in creating a mass style of permanence. Infinitely permeable, its magic rests in the fact that it gave free reign to the imagination and celebrated the fantasies, fears and desires of people all over the world.

86 RIGHT
The Perisphere at the New York World's Fair of 1939. *L'Illustration,* 10 June 1939.
NAL.

TIMELINE

Historical events   Cultural and Artistic events   Key works of Art

1909   Serge Diaghilev moves the Ballets Russes to Paris (until 1929).

Marinetti publishes his Manifesto of Futurism.

1910   George V crowned King of England.

Foundation of the Atelier Martine by Paul Poiret.

1912   Simultaneism launched by Robert and Sonia Delaunay. Salon d'Automne, Paris: presentation of the Maison Cubiste by André Mare and others. First exhibition of the Section d'Or, Paris.

Pablo Picasso's *Still Life with Cane Chair* marks the beginnings of Synthetic Cubism.

1913   Foundation of Primavera workshops, Magasins du Printemps, Paris. The Armory Show, New York. Foundation of the Omega workshops by Roger Fry. The word 'Jazz' first appears in print.

1913–23: Frank Lloyd Wright, Imperial Hotel, Tokyo.

1914   Archduke Franz-Ferdinand of Habsburg murdered in Sarajevo. 28 July: declaration of war.

1917   Abdication of Tsar Nicholas II on 16 March. March to November: Russian Revolution. 6 April: USA enters the war.

Theo Van Doesburg founds De Stijl (until 1928), the Netherlands.

1918   9 November: Weimar Republic. 11 November: Armistice.

1919   28 June: Treaty of Versailles.

Foundation of the Bauhaus in Weimar by Gropius.

1920   1 August: Ghandi starts civil disobedience campaign in India. 10 August: Treaty of Sèvres. End of the Ottoman Empire.

Foundation of *L'Esprit Nouveau* magazine by Le Corbusier, Paul Dermée and Amédée Ozenfant.

1920–22: Armand Rateau designs Jeanne Lanvin's apartment.

1921   Creation of the Communist Party in China by Mao Tse Tung.

1922   31 October: Mussolini assumes power in Italy (March on Rome). 30 December: Lenin declares the creation of the USSR.

Foundation of La Maîtrise workshops, Galeries Lafayette, Paris. Foundation of Pomone workshops, Bon Marché, Paris. *Exposition Nationale et Coloniale, Marseille*. Howard Carter discovers the tomb of Tutankhamun.

Cartier, Egyptian-style jewellery.

1923   Foundation of Studium Louvre workshops, Grands Magasins du Louvre, Paris.

1924   Death of Lenin. Ascension of Stalin. Adolf Hitler, *Mein Kampf.*

1924–25: La Croisière Noire expedition across Africa. Empire Exhibition, Wembley.

Marcel L'Herbier directs the film *L'Inhumaine*. George Gershwin debuts *Rhapsody in Blue*.

1925   *Exposition des Arts Décoratifs et Industriels Modernes*, Paris. *La Revue Nègre* opens in the Music Hall of the Champs Elysées, with Josephine Baker and Sydney Bechet.

Robert Stacy-Judd designs the Aztec Hotel, Monrovia (California).

1926   18 February: report of the discovery of Mayan ruins in Mexico's Yucatan peninsula. Selected works from the Paris 1925 exhibition tour North American cities.

1926–29: Theo van Doesburg designs the Café Aubette, Strasbourg. The Galerie Surréaliste opens in Paris.
Launch of the 'little black dress' by Chanel.

1927   Charles Lindbergh completes the first non-stop aeroplane flight between Paris and New York.

10 January: release of Fritz Lang, *Metropolis*, Berlin. *The Jazz Singer,* the first talkie film, released.

1928   Foundation of the American Union of Decorative Arts and Crafstmen (AUDAC), New York.

Sloane and Robertson, with L. Delamarre and Rene Chambellan, design the Chanin building, New York. 1925–28: Pierre Legrain oversees the design for the studio of Jacques Doucet in Neuilly. Van Alen, Chrysler Building, New York.

1929   Herbert Hoover elected President of the USA. Stock market crash in New York.

Burdekin House Exhibition of Modern Design, Sydney. Foundation of the Union des Artistes Modernes (UAM), Paris.

Shreve, Lamb and Harmon design the Empire State Building, New York. Cecil B. de Mille directs *Dynamite*

1930   Colonial exhibition, Antwerp.

Raymond Hood designs the Rockefeller Center, New York.

1931   *Exposition Coloniale Internationale*, Paris. Rebuilding of Napier, New Zealand. 1931–2: La Croisière Jaune expedition across Asia.

The ocean liner *Empress of Britain* (Canadian Pacific Railways) launched from Southampton. Oliver Bernard completes the Strand Palace Hotel, London. New Palace, Morvi, India, 1931–40. Henri Rapin overseas the design of the Asaka residence, Tokyo. 1924–31: Paul Landowski designs the Monument to Christ the Redeemer, Corcovado peak, Rio de Janeiro.

1932   BBC Broadcasting House, London. *Letty Lynton* with Joan Crawford and *The Mask of Fu Man Chu* with Boris Karloff both released. Sir Owen Williams designs the foyer of the Daily Express building, London.

1933   Century of Progress Exhibition, Chicago. Duke Ellington and his orchestra tour Europe.

Footlight Parade choreographed by Busby Berkeley.

1934   Machine Art exhibition at MoMA, New York.

Bruce Dellit, Anzac Memorial, Hyde Park, Sydney. Cecil B. De Mille, *Cleopatra,* with Claudette Colbert. *The Gay Divorcee* with Ginger Rogers and Fred Astaire.

1935   British Art in Industry Exhibition, London.

The ocean liner *Normandie* launched in St Nazaire, France.

1936   Civil War breaks out in Spain. January: death of George V, Edward VIII crowned King. 10 December: Abdication of Edward VIII.

Empire Exhibition, Johannesburg.

Swing Time with Ginger Rogers and Fred Astaire.

1937   3 June: marriage of Edward and Mrs Simpson.

Exposition Internationale des Arts et Techniques dans la Vie Moderne, Paris. Ideal Home Exhibition, Bombay.

1938   Eros Cinema built in Bombay. Henry Dreyfuss designs the *Twentieth Century Limited* locomotive.

1939   3 September: declaration of war.

Golden Gate Exhibition, San Francisco. World's Fair, New York.

Raymond Hood designs the American Radiator Building, New York.

FURTHER READING

••

KEY TITLES

Arwas, Victor, *The Art of Glass: Art Nouveau to Art Deco* (Windsor, 1996)

Bayer, Patricia, *Art Deco Architecture: Design, Decoration and Detail from the Twenties and Thirties* (London, 1992)

Bayer, Patricia, *Art Deco Interiors: decoration and design classics of the 1920s and 1930s* (London, 1990)

Benton, Charlotte, Benton, Tim, Wood, Ghislaine (ed.), *Art Deco 1910–1939* (London, 2003)

Duncan, Alastair, *American Art Deco* (London, 1986)

Hillier, Bevis and Escritt, Stephen, *Art Deco Style* (London, 1997)

Lussier, Suzanne, *Art Deco Fashion* (London, 2003)

Mandelbaum, Howard and Myers, Eric, *Screen Deco: A Celebration of High Style in Hollywood* (New York and Bromley, 1985)

McCready, Karen, *Art Deco and Modernist Ceramics* (London, 1995)

Raulet, Sylvie, *Art Deco Jewellery* (London, 2002)

Samuels, Charlotte, *Art Deco Textiles* (London, 2003)

JOURNALS

Art et décoration: Revue mensuelle d'art moderne (Paris, 1897–1938)

Art et industrie (Paris, 1909–14, then 1925–54)

Art, goût et beauté (Paris, 1921–33)

Arts et métiers graphiques (Paris, 1927–48)

Die Kunst (Munich, 1899–1940)

Fortune (New York, 1930–)

Good Furniture Magazine (Grand Rapids, Mich., 1925–9)

Harper's Bazar, later known as *Harper's Bazaar* (New York, 1867–)

Kunst und Kunsthandwerk (Vienna, 1898–1924)

La Gazette du bon ton (Paris, 1912–25)

The Home (Sydney, 1920–40)

Studio (London, 1893–1964)

Vogue (New York, 1892–)

Vogue (Paris, 1920–)

PRIMARY MATERIALS

Beaton, Cecil, *The Book of Beauty* (London, 1930)

Bénédictus, Edouard, *Variations* (Paris, 1924)

Bénédictus, Edouard, *Nouvelles variations* (Paris, 1929)

Colin, Paul, *Le Tumulte noir* (Paris, 1927)

Cruège, Pierre, Lajoix, Anne, *René Buthaud, 1886–1986* (Paris, 1996)

Dawes, R. F. C., *A Century of Progress Exhibition: Official View Book* (Chicago, 1933)

Dufrène, Maurice, *Ensembles mobiliers: Exposition internationale de 1925, Séries 1, 2, 3* (Paris, 1925; London, 1989 and 2002)

Fitzgerald, F. Scott, *The Jazz Age* (New York, 1931; 1996)

Herbst, René, *Les Devantures, vitrines, installations de magasins: Exposition internationale de 1925* (Paris, 1925; London, 1927)

Iribe, Paul, *Les Robes de Paul Poiret racontées par Paul Iribe* (Paris, 1908)

Lepape, Georges, *Les Choses de Paul Poiret vues par Georges Lepape* (Paris, 1911)

Magne, Henri-Marcel (ed.), *Rapport général: Exposition des arts décoratifs et industriels modernes*, 12 vols (Paris, 1925–31; reprint, New York, 1977 as Encyclopédie des Arts décoratifs et industriels modernes, 12 vols)

Smith, Hubert Llewellyn and others, *Reports on the Present Position and Tendencies of the Industrial Arts as Indicated at the International Exhibition of Modern Decorative and Industrial Art, Paris, 1925* (London, Department of Overseas Trade, 1925)

The Burdekin House Exhibition: Catalogue (Sydney, 1929)

Vera, André, 'Le Nouveau Style', *L'Art décoratif* (January 1912), pp. 21–32

SECONDARY SOURCES

Albrecht, Donald, *Designing Dreams: Modern Architecture in the Movies* (New York, 1986)

Andrews, Julia F. and Shen, Kuiyi, *A Century in Crisis: Modernity and Tradition in the Art of Twentieth Century China* (exh. cat. Guggenheim Museum; New York, 1998)

Archer-Straw, Petrine, *Negrophilia: Avant Garde Paris and Black Culture in the 1920s* (New York, 2000)

Art Déco na América Latina: 1o Seminário internacional (Rio de Janeiro, 1997)

Arwas, Victor, *Art Deco* (London, 1980; New York, 1992; reprint, New York, 2000)

Arwas, Victor, *Art Deco Sculpture* (London, 1992)

Aynsley, Jeremy, *Graphic Design in Germany, 1890–1945* (London, 2000)

Baker, A. Houston, *Modernism and Harlem Renaissance* (Chicago, 1987)

Battersby, Martin, *The Decorative Thirties* (London, 1971)

Battersby, Martin, *The Decorative Twenties* (London, 1969)

Bibliothèque Nationale de France, *Sonia et Robert Delaunay* (exh. cat. Paris, 1985)

Bonneville, Françoise de, *Jean Puiforcat* (Paris, 1986)

Breunig, LeRoy C. (ed.), *Apollinaire on Art: Essays and Reviews, 1902–1918* (New York and London, 1972; reprint, 1988)

Bröhan, Karl H., *Bröhan-Museum Berlin: Berlin State Museum for Art Nouveau, Art Deco and Functionalism, 1889–1939: Arts, Crafts, Industrial Design, Picture Gallery* (Berlin, 1998)

Brunhammer, Yvonne and Tise, Susan, *The Decorative Arts in France, 1900–1942: La Société des Artistes Décorateurs* (New York, 1990)

Camard, Florence, *Michel Dufet, architecte décorateur* (Paris, 1988)

Camard, Florence, *Ruhlmann, Master of Art Deco* (London, 1984)

Camard, Florence, *Süe et Mare* (Paris, 1993)

Casey, Andrew, *20th Century Ceramic Designers in Britain* (Woodbridge, 2001)

Cerwinske, Laura, Kaye, Danny, *Tropical Deco: the architecture and design of old Miami Beach* (New York, 1981)

Constant, Caroline, *Eileen Gray* (London, 2000)

Curtis, Penelope, *Sculpture 1900–1945: After Rodin*, Oxford, 1999

Damase, Jacques, *Sonia Delaunay: Fashion and Fabrics* (Paris and London, 1991)

Deslandres, Yvonne, *Paul Poiret* (London, 1987)

Duncan, Alastair, *Art Deco Furniture* (London, 1997)

Dwivedi, Sharada and Mehrotra, Rahul, *Bombay: The Cities Within* (Bombay, 1995)

Casey, Andrew and Eatwell, Ann (eds), *Susie Cooper: A Pioneer of Modern Design* (London, 2002)

Eliëns, Titus M., Groot, Marjan and Leidelmeijer, Frans, *Avant Garde Design: Dutch Decorative Arts, 1880–1940* (London, 1997)

Ericsson, Anne-Marie, Ostergard, Derek E., Stritzler-Levine, Nina (ed.), *The Briliance of Swedish Glass, 1918–1939* (exh. cat. Bard Graduate Center for Studies in the Decorative Arts, New Haven and London, 1996)

Fahr-Becker, Gabriele, *Wiener Werkstätte, 1903–1932* (Cologne, 1995)

From Russia with Love: Costumes for the Ballets Russes, 1909–1933 (exh. cat. National Gallery of Australia; Canberra, 1999)

Gaillard, Karin (ed.), *From Neo-Renaissance to Postmodernism: A Hundred and Twenty Years of Dutch Interiors, 1870–1995* (Rotterdam, 1996)

Gary, Marie-Noël de (ed.), *Les Fouquet: Bijoutiers et joailliers à Paris, 1860–1960* (Paris, 1983)

Golan, Romy, *Modernity and Nostalgia: French Art and Politics between the Wars* (New Haven and London, 1995)

Greenhalgh, Paul, *Quotations and Sources on Design and the Decorative Arts* (Manchester, 1993)

Greenhalgh, Paul (ed.), *Modernism in Design* (London, 1990, repr.1997)

Gronberg, Tag, *Designs on Modernity: Exhibiting the City in 1920s Paris* (Manchester and New York, 1998)

Guillaume, Valérie, *Europe, 1910-1939: Quand l'art habillait le vêtement* (Paris, 1997)

Hanks, David A., Toher, Jennifer, *Donald Deskey: decorative designs and interiors* (New York, 1987)

Hambourg, Maria Morris and Phillips, Christopher, *The New Vision: Photography between the World Wars: Ford Motor Company Collection at the Metropolitan Museum of Art, New York* (exh. cat. Metropolitan Museum of Art; New York, 1989)

Haskell, Barbara, *American Century: Art and Culture, 1900–1950* (exh. cat. Whitney Museum of American Art, New York, 1999)

Heller, Steven and Fili, Louise, *Italian Art Deco Graphic Design between the Wars* (San Francisco, 1993)

Hillier, Bevis, *Art Deco of the Twenties and Thirties* (London, 1968)

Hillier, Bevis, *The World of Art Deco* (exh. cat. Minneapolis Institute of Art; Minneapolis and London, 1971)

Holmes, Fred and Newton Holmes, Ann, *Bridging Traditions: The making of Umaid Bhawan Palace* (Delhi, 1995)

Ingle, Marjorie I., *The Mayan Revival Style: Art Deco Mayan Fantasy* (Salt Lake City, 1984)

Johnson, J. Stewart, *American Modern, 1925–1940: Design for a New Age* (New York, 2000)

Kahr, Joan, *Edgar Brandt: Master of Art Deco Ironwork* (New York, 1999)

Kaplan, Wendy (ed.), *'Designing Modernity': The Arts of Reform and Persuasion, 1885–1945* (London, 1995)

Kery, Patricia Frantz, *Art Deco Graphics* (London, 1986)

Klein, Dan, McClelland, Nancy and Haslam, Malcolm, *In the Deco Style* (London, 1987)

L'Ecotais, Emmanuelle de and Sayag, Alain, *Man Ray: Photography and its Double* (Paris and London, 1998)

Lemke, Sieglinde, *Primitivist Modernism: Black Culture and the Origins of Transatlantic Modernism* (Oxford, 1998)

Licitra Ponti, Lisa, *Gio Ponti: The Complete Work, 1923–1978* (London, 1990)

Lambreths, Marc (ed.), *L'Art Déco en Europe* (exh. cat. Palais des Beaux-Arts; Brussels, 1989)

Mansbach, Steven A., *Modern Art in Eastern Europe* (Cambridge, 1999)

McFadden, David Revere (ed.), *Scandinavian Modern Design, 1880–1980* (exh. cat. Cooper-Hewitt Museum; New York, 1982)

Marcilhac, Félix, *Jean Dunand: His Life and Works* (London, 1991)

Marcilhac, Félix, *René Lalique 1860–1945, maître verrier: analyse de l'oeuvre et catalogue raisonné* (Paris, 1989)

Mendes, Valerie, *British Textiles from 1900 to 1937* (London, 1992)

Michell, George, *The Royal Palaces of India* (London, 1994)

Nadelhoffer, Hans, *Cartier: Jewellers Extraordinary* (London, 1984)

Opie, Jennifer Hawkins and Hollis, Marianne, *Thirties: British Art and Design before the War* (London, 1979)

Pérez Rojas, J., *Art Déco en España* (Madrid, 1990)

Possémé, Evelyne, *1910–1930: Les Années 1925, Musée des Arts Décoratifs* (Paris, 1999)

Powell, Richard J. and Bailey, David A., *Rhapsodies in Black: Art of the Harlem Renaissance* (Exh. Cat. Hayward Gallery, London, 1997)

Rohatgi, Pauline and others, *Bombay to Mumbai: Changing Perspectives* (Bombay, 1997)

Rudoe, Judy, *Cartier, 1900–1939* (London, 1997)

Selkurt, Claire, 'New Classicism: Design of the 1920s in Denmark', *Journal of Decorative and Propaganda Arts*, vol. 4 (Spring 1987), pp. 16–29

Sklar, Robert, *Movie Made Cinema: A Cultural History of American Movies* (New York, 1975)

Stewart, David B., *The Making of a Modern Japanese Architecture: 1868 to the Present* (Tokyo and New York, 1987)

Troy, Nancy, *Modernism and the Decorative Arts in France: Art Nouveau to Le Corbusier* (New Haven and London, 1991)

Umlĕckoprůmyslové Muzeum v Praze, *Czech Art Deco, 1918–1938* (exh. cat. Palazzo della Ragione, Padua; Milan, 1996; Municipal Museum, Prague, 1998)

Van Daele, Patrick and Lumby, Roy, *A Spirit of Progress: Art Deco Architecture in Australia* (Sydney, 1997)

Völker, Angela and Pichler, Rupert, *Textiles of the Wiener Werkstätte* (Vienna, 1990; London, 1994)

Vreeland, Diana, *D.V.* (New York, 1985)

Wichmann, Hans, *Design contra Art Déco, 1927–1932: Jahrfünft der Wende* (Munich, 1993)

Wilson Richard Guy and others, *The Machine Age in America, 1918–1941* (exh. cat. Brooklyn Museum; New York, 1986)

Zignani, Federico, *A journey through American Art Deco: Architecture, Design and Cinemas in the Twenties and Thirties* (Seattle, 1997)

NOTES

••••••••••••••••••••••••••••••••

1 F. Scott Fitzgerald, *The Jazz Age,* first published in 1931; (New York, 1996), p.3.

2 Quoted in Charlotte Benton, Tim Benton and Ghislaine Wood (eds), *Art Deco 1910–1939,* (London, 2003), p.16.

3 Quoted in Paul Greenhalgh, *Quotations and Sources on Design and the Decorative Arts,* (Manchester, 1993), p.111.

4 F. Scott Fitzgerald, *The Jazz Age,* first published in 1931; (New York, 1996), p.5.

5 Guillaume Apollinaire, 1912, in *Apollinaire on Art: Essays and Reviews 1902–1918,* edited by Leroy C. Breunig, (New York, 1972), p.208.

6 Guillaume Apollinaire, 'African and Oceanic sculptures', Les Arts à Paris, 15 July 1918, in *Apollinaire on Art: Essays and Reviews 1902–1918,* edited by Leroy C. Breunig, (New York, 1972), p.470.

7 Roger Fry, in *Art Now* by Herbert Read, first published in 1933; (London, 1960), p.79.

8 Quoted in Paul Greenhalgh, *Quotations and Sources on Design and the Decorative Arts,* (Manchester, 1993), p.20.

9 Quoted in Fritz Lang, *Metropolis, Cinematic Visions of Technology and Fear,* edited by Michael Minden and Holger Brachman, (Rochester, 2000), p.4.

10 Paul T. Frankl, *New Dimensions: The Decorative Arts of Today in Words & Pictures,* (New York, 1928), p.61.

11 Quoted in Richard Wilson, Diane Pilgrim, Dickran Tashjian, *The Machine Age in America 1918–1941,* (New York, 1986), p.308.

PICTURE CREDITS

••••••••••••••••••••••••••••••••

Plate 2
Photo: Laurent-Sully Jaulmes. © ADAGP, Paris and DACS, London 2002.

Plates 4 and 56
Photo: CNAC/MNAM – Dist. RMN. © ADAGP, Paris and DACS, London 2002.

Plates 6, 19, 24, 30, 37, 48, 53
© ADAGP, Paris and DACS, London 2002.

Plate 9
© Photo: Antonio Martinelli.

Plate 10
Collection Tour Eiffel, Paris.

Plate 11
Photo: Katherine Wetzel.

Plate 12
© Photo: Romilly Lockyer/Getty Images/ The Image Bank.

Plate 20
Conner • Rosenkranz, New York.

Plates 21 and 59
© DACS 2002.

Plates 23 and 67
Photo: Miloslav Sebek.

Plate 26
© PMVP. Photo: Pierrain.

Plate 36
Photo: Patrick van Daele.

Plate 39
Photo: Nick Welsh. © Cartier.

Plate 41
© Crown Copyright. NMR.

Plate 42
BFI Stills, Posters and Designs. Courtesy of Universal Studios Licensing LLLP.

Plate 45
Photo: Edgar Harden.

Plate 47
Christie's Images Ltd. © Cartier.

Plate 51
Photo: Anthony Israel. © ADAGP, Paris and DACS, London 2002.

Plates 55, 65, 66, 72 and 79
Courtesy Museum of Fine Arts, Boston.

Plate 57
© L&M Services B.V. Amsterdam 20020914.

Plate 60 and back jacket illustration
Christie's Images Ltd. © ADAGP, Paris and DACS, London 2002.

Plate 69
© English Heritage, NMR.

Plate 75
Photo: Cathy Carver.

Plate 76
Photo: Dennis Cowley.

Plate 78
© Christie's Images Ltd 2000.

Plate 82
Photo: Tim Benton.

Plate 86
Photo: René Bras.

INDEX

••

Page numbers in italic refer to the illustration captions on those pages.